Oodles of Noodles

comfort activities and more...

GF–18, Virat Bhavan
Commercial Complex, Mukherjee Nagar
Delhi 110009
Phone: +91-11-47038000 / Fax: +91-11-47038099
Email orders or enquiries: info@offshootbooks.com

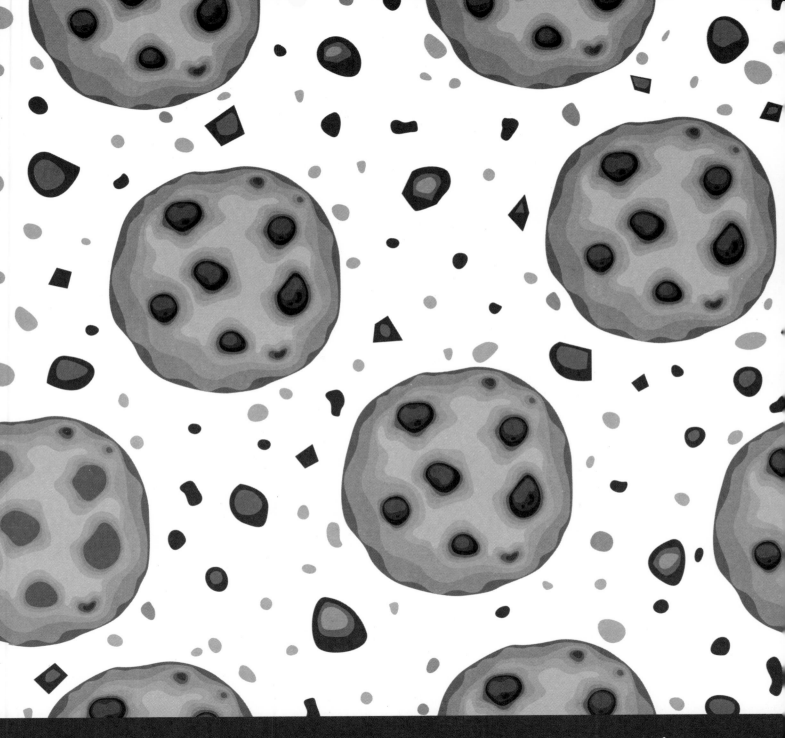

Choco-chip, choco-chip—count them before you flip.

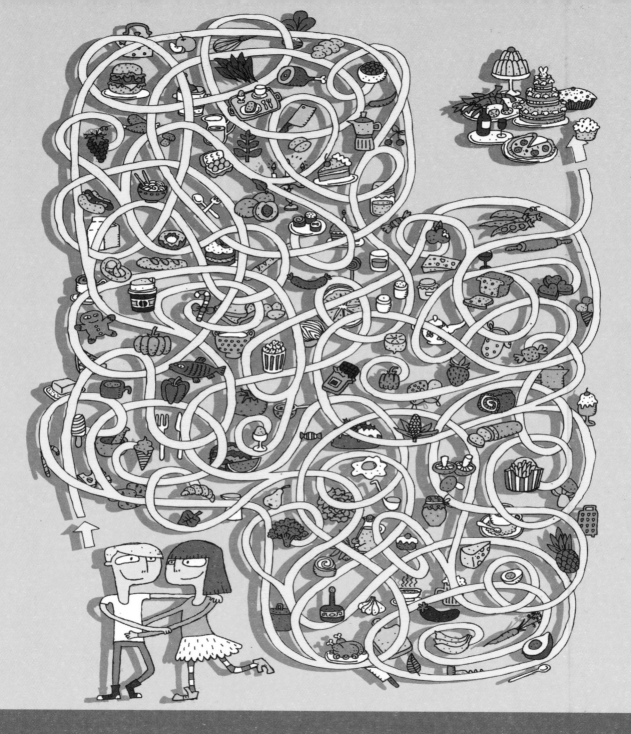

Help them find their way to their favorite food.

Across

2 Want to smile? Just say _____
5 The rookie wants to have a _____
7 Crispy things, have them with syrup or butter
8 As flat as a _____
9 A nutter butter

Down

1 Ravioli, spaghetti, fusilli are all kinds of _____
2 A cup of this is enough to make everything seem better
3 Sweet, usually brown, mostly sold as a block
4 A food in the form of long, thin strands; everyone loves these
6 Small tube-shaped Italian invention

Comforting crossword!

DRINK

FOOD

DESSERT

TGIF! That's what the menu would be.

Add color to the crumbling cookies!

Some are happy; some are sad. Color them all—none should feel bad.

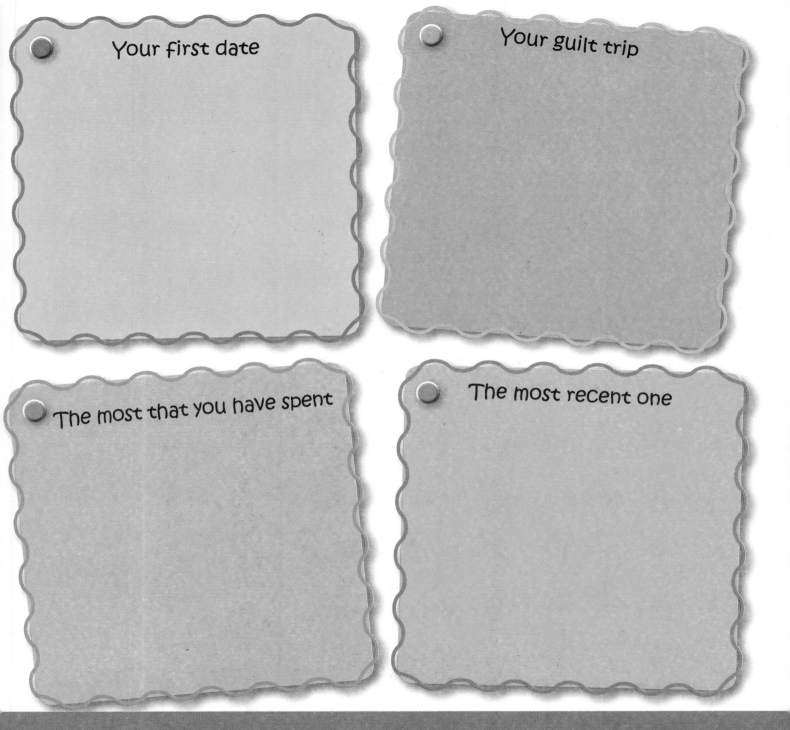

Your first date

Your guilt trip

The most that you have spent

The most recent one

You have been billed.

Huff-ing and puff-ing—count the people in the muffin.

Make it a pretty sight—color and make it bright.

Halloween—find my twin!

 **CHEESEBURGER**
USA

 **TACOS**
_____

 **FISH AND CHIPS**
_____

 **CURRY**
_____

 **PIZZA**
_____

 **GREEK SALAD**
_____

 **PRETZEL**
_____

 **SUSHI**
_____

 **TOM YUM KUNG**
_____

 **DUMPLINGS**
_____

 **JAMON**
_____

 **PANCAKES**
_____

 **CROISSANT**
_____

 **PAELLA**
_____

 **SAUSAGE**
_____

NASI GORENG
_____

That's where we belong!

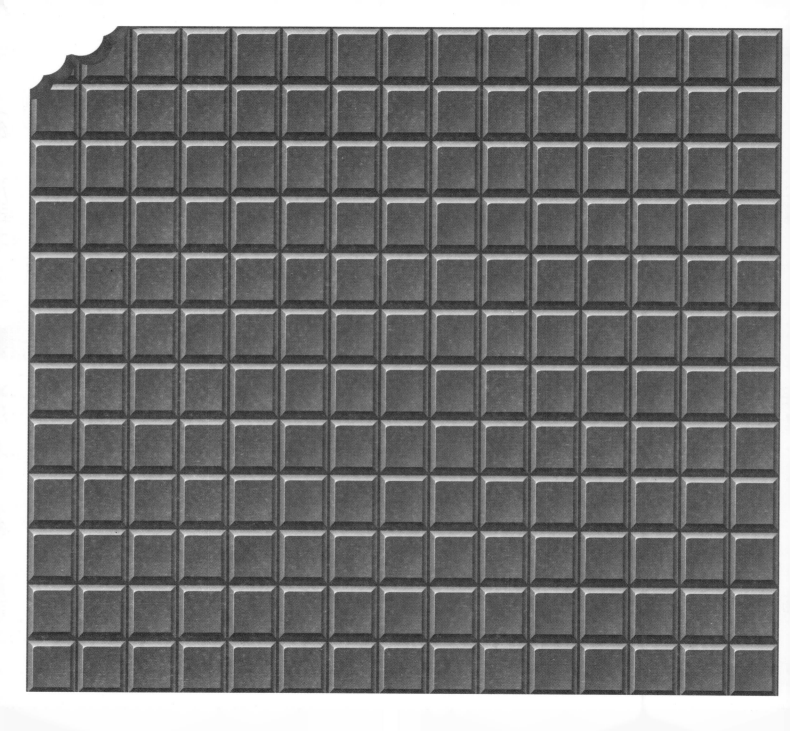

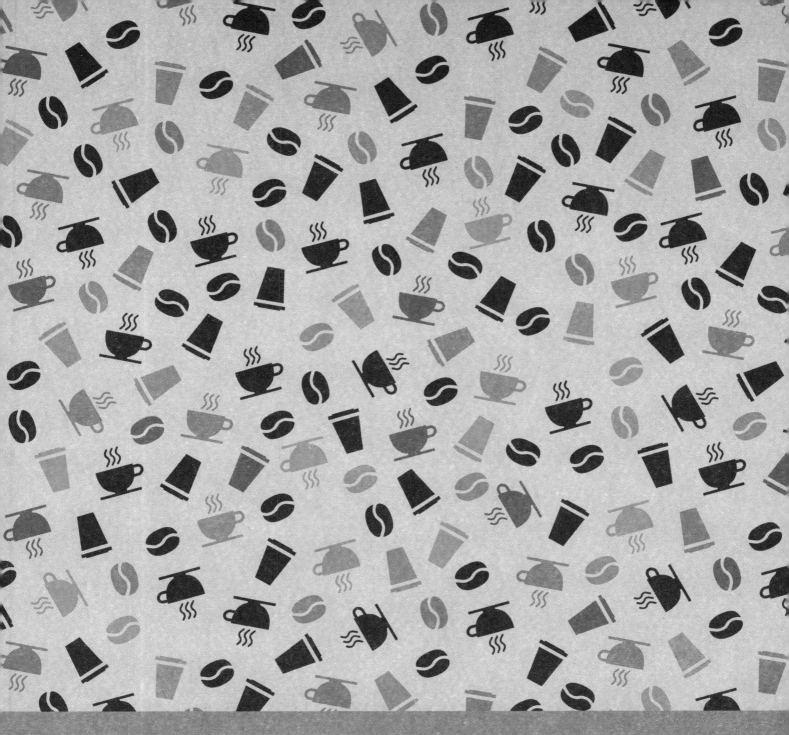

Count everything that's coffee.

Lap the cap—of all your favorite drinks!

Make your own bar!

Doodle your silver meal!

Who's getting my food, dude?

I want a refill!

Parmigiano-Reggiano
ankimo cupcakes Emmental
Gouda Camembert
macaronienchilada
halibut buttermilk croissant
hummus parm mustard Taleggio
Goetta dumplings coffee Pizza
Feta fondu sandwich tofubagel Lasagna
Pepperoni pho marzipan crab fajita sausage Waffles
chicken oreo som Cotija
cocoa cake stinky salami eggrolls
chilli ketchup tam
gnocchi Roquefort frenchpretzel toast doughnut
Meatballs salad poutine curry tacos
Manchego Yogurt chutney sushi kale pancakes
Chèvre pancakes Pasta
Burger pepperonichamp
Cheddar chocolate
Mozzarella
Monterey Jack

Say cheese! Thirteen, please!

Don't mumble and grumble—find the foods in the jungle.

How many champagne flutes? Color them in colors of different fruits

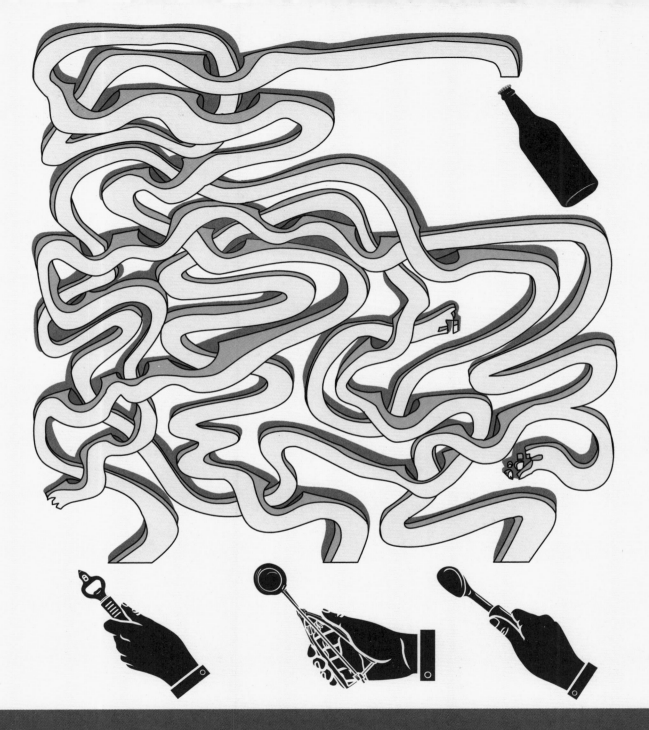

And the right opener is...

Odd one out! Find it—without a doubt!

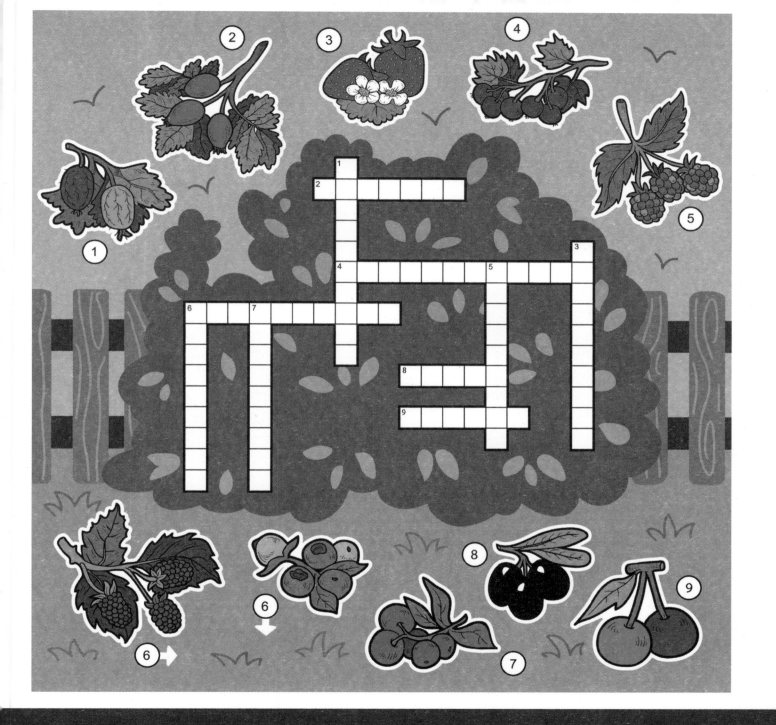

Berry-berry Crosswordy!

Food is the color of thin lines!

Monday

Tuesday

Wednesday

Thursday

Friday

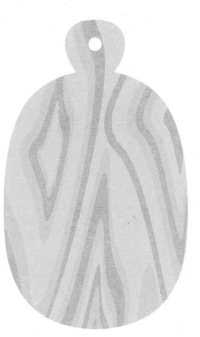

Saturday

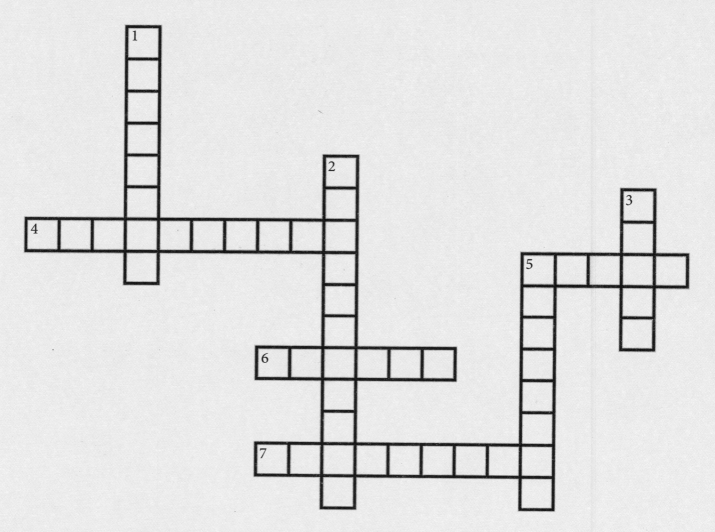

ACROSS

4. French word for a bakery

5. Type of pastry used to make profiteroles

6. Green horseradish in Japan

7. Author of *Charlie and the Chocolate Factory*

DOWN

1. Food of the gods in Greek mythology

2. Caesar Cardini's gift to the culinary world

3. What are Pershore eggs and Marjorie's seedlings?

5. Drink invented by John Pemberton

The foody crossword.

PLEASE
DONUT
DISTURB

Book it!

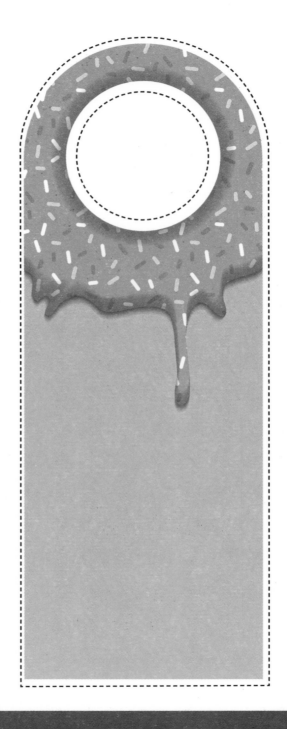

Book it!

Color me bright!

Help the foodie reach her love!

Ice creams I crave-err—and these are my favorite flavors!

It's all in my mind! But in this jumble, you find.

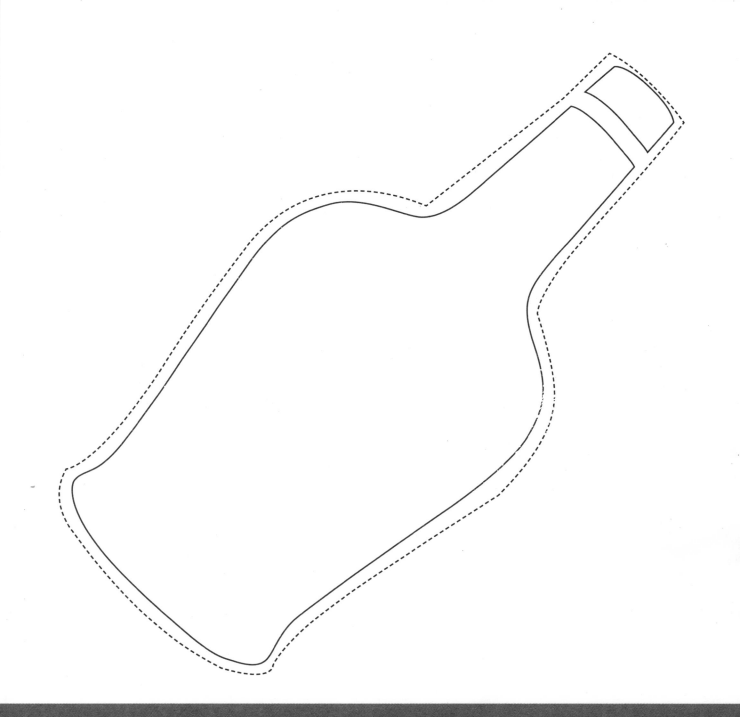

Book it! Doodle—color—use!

Don't whine, just wine!

Book it!

This time it's odd and not even—find differences seven.

Screw the cork!

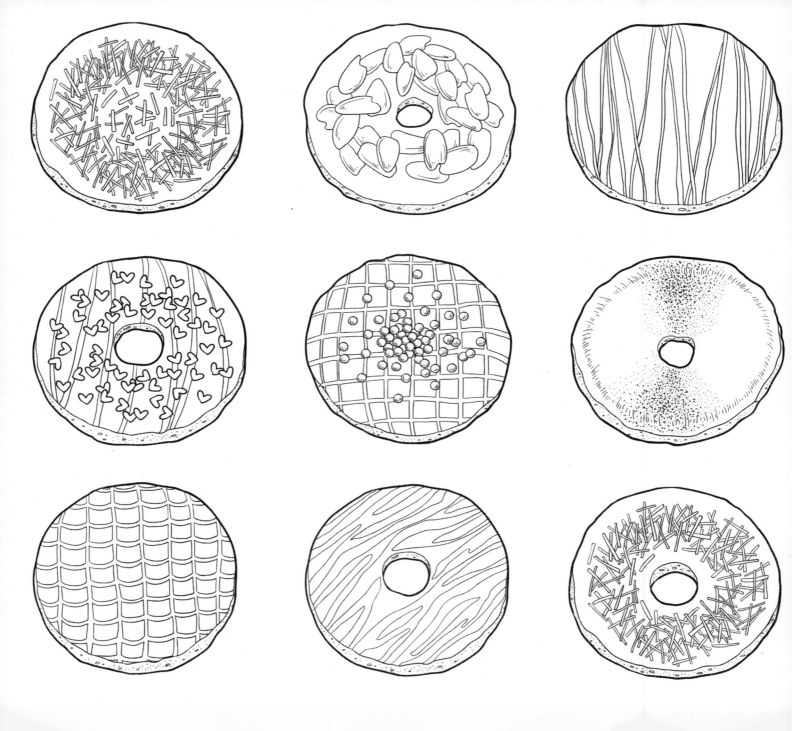

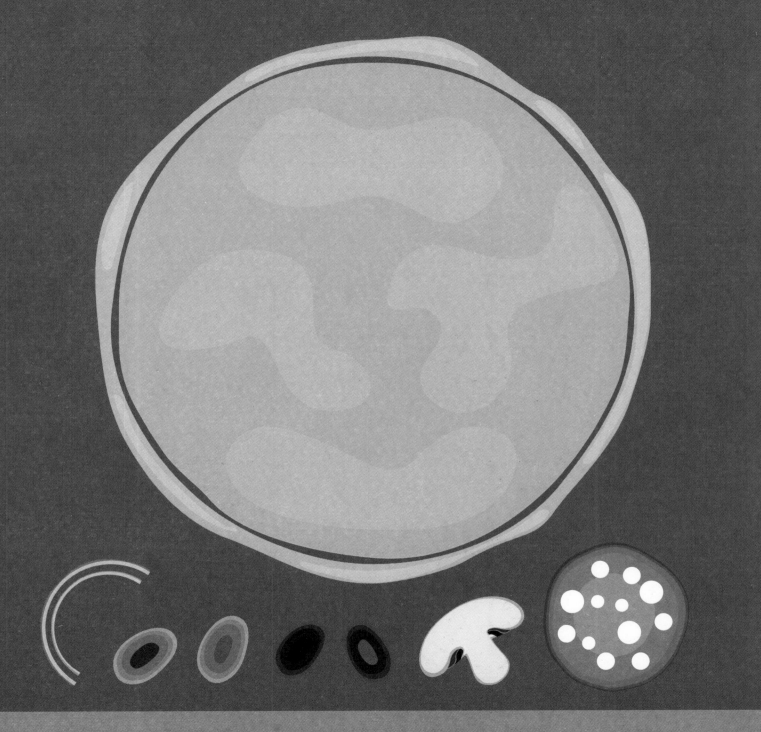

No more chopping—doodle your favorite pizza toppings!

Without investing a buck, design your own food truck!

That's a tall one. Find what's missing and you're done.

Too drunk to find one?

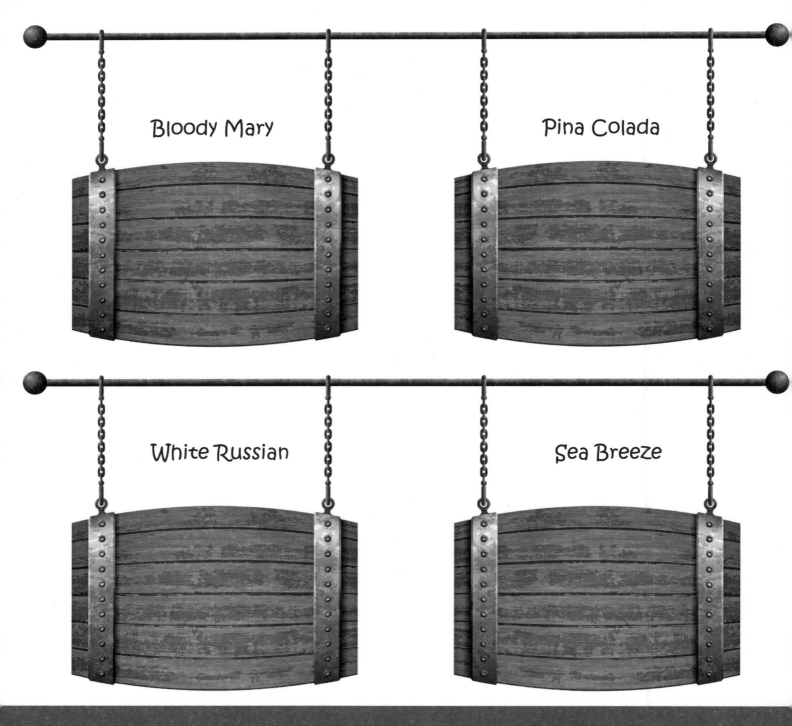

Bloody Mary

Pina Colada

White Russian

Sea Breeze

Raise your glass! List down the ingredients of these cool cocktails.

Made in heaven are differences seven!

Toast with eggs and bacon—what breakfast today had you taken?

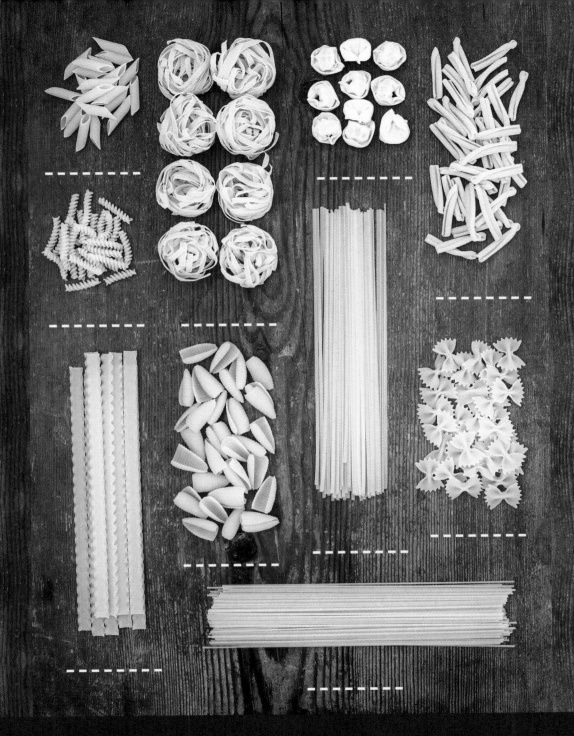

Are you a foodie? Naming these pastas wouldn't be a difficulty.

For a splash of color each begs, make your own easter eggs.

That's a lot of shopping to do!

Italian restaurant

Color all things Italian.

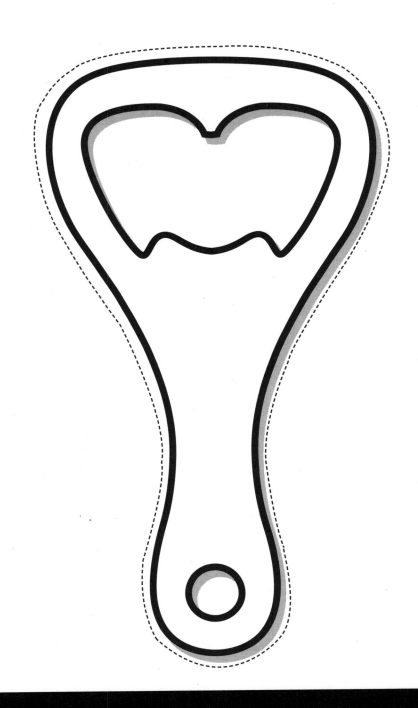

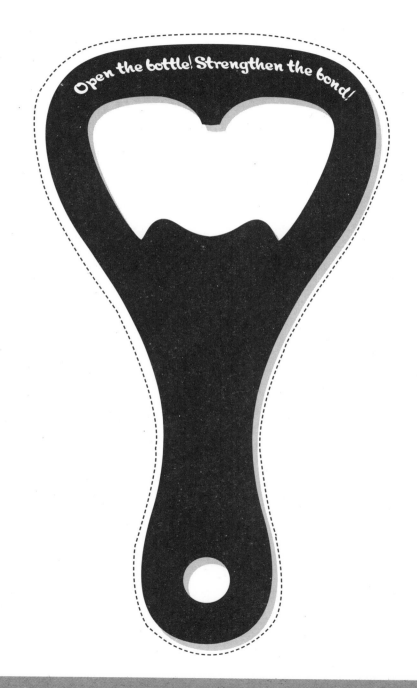

Open the bottle! Strengthen the bond!

Book it!

Life without a waffle is awful! Make your own.

On the paper glue your eyes—concentrate and count the fries.

More cubes. More bars. Bounty, Tob and Mars.

Tea Time

_____

_____

_____

_____

_____

_____

Su-Do-Ku!
So-Do-We!

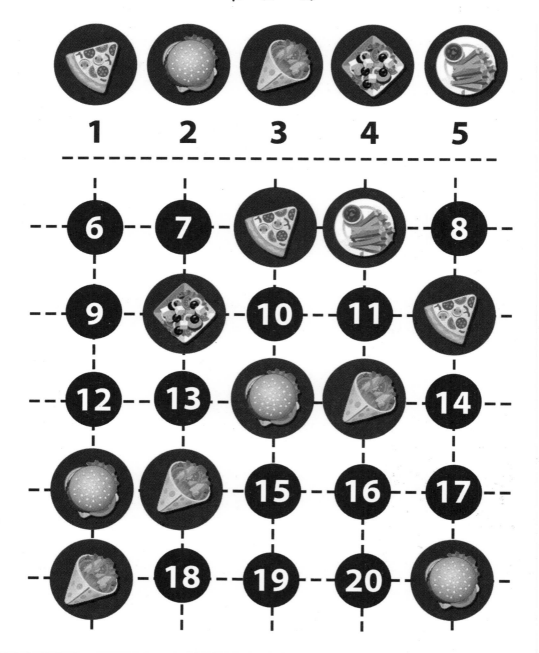

Fill in the blanks using the pictures given above. When you finish, there should be only one of each picture in a row and in a column.

That looks like a lot! Trace who's eating what.

Answer: 87

Comforting Crossword

ACROSS	DOWN
2. Cheese	1. Pasta
5. Cookie	2. Coffee
7. Waffles	3. Chocolate
8. Pancake	4. Noodles
9. Peanut butter	6. Macaroni

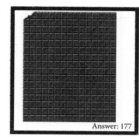

Answer: 269

Answer: 2, 11

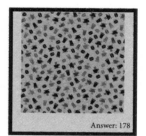

Answer: 177

Answer: 178

Answer: 6

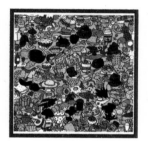

Answer:

1. Gooseberry 2. Rosehip 3. Strawberry
4. Blackcurrant 5. Raspberry
6. (across) Blackberry 6. (down) Blueberry
7. Cranberry 8. Olive 9. Cherry

Knife to peel
Puntilla knife
Cleaner knife
Knife to carve
Salmon knife
Spatula
Fork to carve

Vegetables knife
Cutlet knife
Knife to fillet
Cook knife
Jam knife
Bread knife
Santoku knife

The Foody Crossword

7. Roald Dahl
4. Patisserie
2. Caesar salad
5. Coca Cola
6. Wasabi
1. Ambrosia
5. Choux
3. Plums

SAUTE   GRILL   CHOP

STIR   SEASON   DEEP FRY

Answer: 3

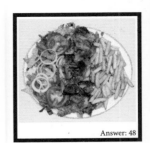

Answer: 48

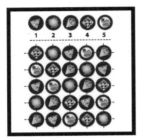

Answer:

grandpa - mushrooms

son - french fries

father - pizza

baby - carrot

mother - watermelon

daughter - cake

grandma - cheese